Elegant
IRIS
Folding

Gefeliciteerd

Maruscha Gaasenbeek
Tine Beauveser

FORTE PUBLISHERS

Contents

ISBN 90 5877 322 1
NUR 475

This is a publication from
Forte Publishers BV
P.O. Box 1394
3500 BJ Utrecht
The Netherlands

For more information about the creative books available from Forte Publishers:
www.hobby-party.com

Publisher: Marianne Perlot
Editor: Hanny Vlaar
Photography and digital image editing: Fotografie Gerhard Witteveen, Apeldoorn, the Netherlands
Cover and inner design: BADE creatieve communicatie, Baarn, the Netherlands
Layout: Elgraphic+DTQP, Schiedam, the Netherlands
Translation: TextCase Book Productions, Michael Ford

Foreword

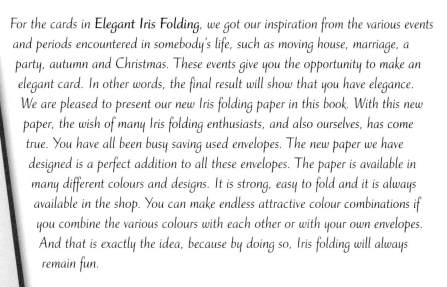

For the cards in **Elegant Iris Folding**, we got our inspiration from the various events and periods encountered in somebody's life, such as moving house, marriage, a party, autumn and Christmas. These events give you the opportunity to make an elegant card. In other words, the final result will show that you have elegance. We are pleased to present our new Iris folding paper in this book. With this new paper, the wish of many Iris folding enthusiasts, and also ourselves, has come true. You have all been busy saving used envelopes. The new paper we have designed is a perfect addition to all these envelopes. The paper is available in many different colours and designs. It is strong, easy to fold and it is always available in the shop. You can make endless attractive colour combinations if you combine the various colours with each other or with your own envelopes. And that is exactly the idea, because by doing so, Iris folding will always remain fun.

We wish you lots of fun with **Elegant Iris Folding!**

Maruscha   Tine

Thanks: Hermien and Ina from Ugchelen for your pretty, creative spruces.

Techniques

The starting point for Iris folding is the pattern. Cut the outer shape of the pattern out of the card and then fill the hole from the outside to the inside with folded strips of used envelopes and/or Iris folding paper. You work at the back of the card, so you work, in fact, on a mirror image. When you have finished the Iris folding, stick the card onto another card. For a pentagon pattern, select five different pieces of paper where the patterns and colours combine and contrast each other nicely. Cut or fold all the paper into strips in the same way, for example, from left to right. The number of different strips you will need depends on the pattern; you will need between four and eight strips. The width of the strips also depends on the pattern and is stated for each card. You must first fold the edge of the strips over and then sort them into each different type of paper. Next, cover each section in turn by following the numbers (1, 2, 3, 4, 5, etc.), so that the pattern is continuously rotated. Lay the strips down with the fold facing towards the middle of the pattern and stick the left and right-hand sides to the card using adhesive tape. Finally, use an attractive piece of deco tape or holographic paper to cover the hole in the middle.

The pentagon

The most important thing is to start with the *basic pentagon*, because, from this, you will learn the unique folding and sticking technique needed for all the patterns. You will notice that you quickly get used to the technique of Iris folding.

Preparation

1. Lay the smallest card down (*Step-by-step*: 13.1 x 9.7 cm, yellow) with the back facing towards you.
2. Use a light box to copy the circumference of the pentagon onto the card and cut it out.
3. Punch out the corners of the yellow card using the diamond corner punch.
4. Stick a copy of the basic pentagon given in this book (pattern 1) on your cutting mat using adhesive tape.
5. Place the card with the hole on top of the pattern (you should be looking at the back of the card) and only stick the left-hand side of the card to your cutting mat using masking tape.
6. Choose five different sheets of Iris folding paper with different patterns. Five different pieces of Iris folding paper from the orange set have been used for the card on page 5.
7. Cut *2 cm wide* strips from these sheets and make separate piles of colour A, colour B, colour C, colour D and colour E.
8. Fold a border (approximately 7 mm wide) along the entire length of each strip with *the nice side facing outwards*.

1. All 64 colours from the eight new sets of Iris folding paper.

2. Cut out the pentagon from the back of the single card.

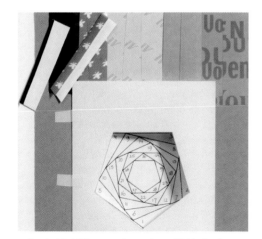

3. Cut the Iris folding paper into strips and fold a border along the entire length of each strip. Stick the pattern to your cutting mat, place the card on top of it and tape the left-hand side to the cutting mat.

4. Place the strips exactly against the line and stick down the left and right-hand sides using adhesive tape. Fold the card open from time to time to see whether the pattern continues nicely.

Iris folding

9. Take a folded strip of colour A and place it over section 1, exactly against the line of the pattern with the folded edge facing towards the middle. Allow 0.5 cm to stick out on the left and right-hand sides and cut the rest off.
10. Stick the left and right-hand sides of the strip to the card using a small piece of adhesive tape, but remain approximately 0.5 cm from the edge of the card.
11. Take a strip of colour B and place it on section 2 of the pattern. Tape the left and right-hand sides to the card.
12. Take a strip of colour C. Place this on section 3 and stick it into place.
13. Take a strip of colour D. Place this on section 4 and stick it into place.
14. Take a strip of colour E. Place this on section 5 and stick it into place.
15. Continue with colour A on section 6, colour B on section 7, colour C on section 8, colour D on section 9 and colour E on section 10. The strips on sections 1, 6, 11, 16, 21 and 26 of this pattern are all of colour A. The strips on sections 2, 7, 12, 17, 22 and 27 are all of colour B. The strips on sections 3, 8, 13, 18, 23 and 28 are all of colour C. The strips on sections 4, 9, 14, 19, 24 and 29 are all of colour D. The strips on sections 5, 10, 15, 20, 25 and 30 are all of colour E.

Finishing

After finishing section 30, carefully remove the card. Stick a piece of holographic paper in the middle on the back of the card. Stick double-sided adhesive tape around the edge of the card, remove the protective layer and stick the Iris folding pattern on brown card (13.7 x 10.2 cm) and then on a mango double card. Do not use glue, because all the paper strips place pressure on the card.

Embossing

To emboss, place the stencil on the good side of the card and stick it in place using masking tape. Place the card (with the stencil) upside-down on a light box. Carefully push the paper through the stencil's opening using the embossing pen. You only have to push along the edges to raise the entire image.

Using text sheets

Cut the A4 text sheet into four and use the piece which suits the other pieces of paper best. Leave the first text line and cut the second line horizontally through the middle. Leave the third text line and cut the fourth line through the middle. This will produce approximately 1.6 cm wide strips which you can use instead of a group of envelope strips. When working *at the top* of a pattern, fold the coloured border under the text. To make a straight fold, score a line on the back of the strip using a ruler.

Materials

To make the cards:

- ❏ Card: Canson Mi-Teintes (C), Artoz (A) and Papicolor (P)
- ❏ Iris folding text stickers
- ❏ Knife
- ❏ Cutting mat
- ❏ Ruler with a metal cutting edge (Securit)
- ❏ Adhesive tape
- ❏ Double-sided adhesive tape
- ❏ Masking tape
- ❏ Various punches (TomTas, Make me!, Carl and Picture Punch)
- ❏ Corner punches (Fiskars, Reuser, TomTas, Carl)
- ❏ Border ornament punches (Fiskars)
- ❏ Punch with exchangeable shapes (TomTas)
- ❏ Various embossing stencils (Marianne Design, Linda Design, Erica Fortgens)
- ❏ Scissors and silhouette scissors
- ❏ Gel pen
- ❏ Pencil
- ❏ Corner scissors (Fiskars)
- ❏ Photo glue
- ❏ Light box

Iris folding

- ❏ Iris folding paper
- ❏ Used envelopes
- ❏ Origami paper
- ❏ Iris folding text and greetings sheets
- ❏ Deco tape
- ❏ Holographic paper

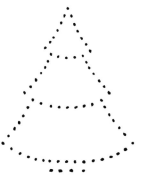

Spruce embroidery pattern

The patterns

Full-size examples of all the patterns are given in this book. Draw round the outside of the shape using a light box. The shapes are easy to cut out of the card using either a knife or a pair of scissors. Special cut-out cards are available for the basket, the rose and the Christmas decoration.

Pentagons

Glittering colours from the eight new sets of Iris folding paper.

All the cards are made according to the instructions given for the basic pentagon (see Techniques). For cards 1, 5, 6 and 8, turn the pentagon pattern so that the bottom of the pattern is horizontal.

Card 1

Card: purple P13 (14.8 x 21 cm) and pale pink C103 (13.4 x 9.4 cm) • Pattern 1 • 2 cm wide strips from 5 sheets of the purple Iris folding paper set • Silver holographic paper • Diamond corner scissors
Cut the pentagon out of the small card and punch out the corners.

Card 2

Card: green A309 (14.8 x 21 cm) and silver-grey P02 (13.8 x 9.5 cm) • Pattern 1 • 2 cm wide strips from 5 sheets of the green Iris folding paper set • Silver holographic paper • Art Deco corner scissors
Cut the pentagon out of the small card. Cut the corners using the corner scissors.

Card 3 – Basic pattern

Card: mango A575 (14.8 x 21 cm), Havana C502 (13.7 x 10.2 cm) and lemon yellow C101 (13.1 x 9.7 cm) • Pattern 1 • 2 cm wide strips from 5 sheets of the orange Iris folding paper set • Gold holographic paper • Diamond corner punch

Card 4

Card: light blue C102 (14.8 x 21 cm and 13.5 x 9.5 cm) and azure C590 (14 x 10 cm) • Pattern 1 • 2 cm wide strips from 5 sheets of the blue Iris folding paper set • Silver holographic paper • Regal corner scissors

Card 5

Card: dark chestnut C501 (14.8 x 21 cm) and white C335 (12.3 x 9.5 cm) • Piece of ochre Iris folding paper (13.2 x 9.8 cm) from the yellow Iris folding paper set • Pattern 1 • 2 cm wide strips from 5 sheets of the yellow Iris folding paper set • Gold holographic paper • Art Deco corner scissors

Card 6

Card: turquoise P32 (14.8 x 21 cm) and pearl grey C120 (13.5 x 9.5 cm) • Piece of paper (14 x 10 cm) from the aqua Iris folding paper set • Pattern 1 • 2 cm wide strips from 5 sheets of the aqua Iris folding paper set • Silver holographic paper • Diamond corner punch

Card 7

Card: pale pink C103 (14.8 x 21 cm and 13.8 x 9.5 cm) • Piece of red paper A519 (13.8 x 9.5 cm) • Pattern 1 • 2 cm wide strips from 5 sheets of the red Iris folding paper set • Silver holographic paper • Art Deco corner scissors

Card 8

Card: pastel green A331 (14.8 x 21 cm), dark green A309 (14.2 x 9.7 cm) and white C335 (13.7 x 9.5 cm) • Pattern 1 • 2 cm wide strips from 5 sheets of the petrol Iris folding paper set • Silver holographic paper • Diamond corner punch

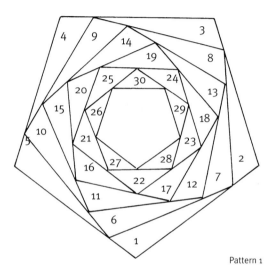

Pattern 1

Playing with pentagons

Congratulations with your new house!

All the houses are made according to the instructions given for card 1.

Card 1

Card: salmon C384 (14.8 x 21 cm) and white (14 x 9.6 cm) • Pattern 2 • 2 cm wide strips from 5 red, purple, orange and grey envelopes • Piece of grey paper (5 x 7 cm) for the roof • Silver holographic paper • Text stickers • Carl corner punch

Cut the house, without the roof, out of the small card and punch out the corners. Fill the pattern as described for the basic technique. Cut the roof and the chimney out of the piece of grey paper and stick them on the card with the text stickers.

Card 2

Card: warm yellow C553 (14.8 x 21 cm) and white C335 (13.8 x 9.5 cm) • Pattern 2 • 2 cm wide strips from 5 sheets of the orange Iris folding paper set • Piece of brown Iris folding paper (5 x 7 cm) for the roof • Gold holographic paper • Bronze gel pen • Multi-corner punch

Pattern 2

Card 3

*Card: yellow-pink C350 (14.8 x 21 cm) and green
A339 (13.8 x 9.5 cm) • Pattern 2 • 5 groups of
2 cm wide strips from 3 brown, grey and pink
envelopes • Piece of grey paper (5 x 7 cm) for the
roof • Gold holographic paper • Text sticker •
Leaves 3-in-1 corner punch*

Card 4

*Card: chestnut C501 (14.8 x 21 cm) and beige
(13.8 x 9.5 cm) • Pattern 2 • 2 cm wide strips from
the orange Iris folding paper set and 3 different
blue and brown envelopes • Piece of brown Iris
folding paper (5 x 7 cm) for the roof • Gold
holographic paper • Text sticker • Gel pen •
Flowers 3-in-1 corner punch*

Card 5

*Card: earth red C130 (14.8 x 21 cm) and white
C335 (13.8 x 9.5 cm) • Pattern 2 • 2 cm wide strips
from 5 sheets of the orange Iris folding paper set
• Piece of brown paper (5 x 7 cm) for the roof •
Gold holographic paper • Text sticker • Bronze gel
pen • Multi-corner punch*

Card 6

Card: dark green A309 (14.8 x 21 cm) and white C335 (13.3 x 9.5 cm) • Pattern 2 • 2 cm wide strips from 5 sheets of the petrol Iris folding paper set • Piece of petrol Iris folding paper (5 x 7 cm) for the roof • Text sticker • Grass hand punch • Wave border ornament punch

Duo and diamond

A wedding, moving in together, an
anniversary: they all deserve a card.

The duo card is made according to the
description given for card 1. The diamond
card is made according to the description
given for card 3.

Card 1 (on the cover)

Card: rust C504 (14.8 x 21 cm), wine red C503
(13.7 x 9.8 cm) and carnation white P03
(13.4 x 9.4 cm) • Pattern 3 • 2 cm wide strips from
3 sheets of the red Iris folding paper set • Copper
deco tape • Multi-corner punch
Cut the triangles out of the small card and punch
out two corners.

Card 2

Card: brick red C505 (14.8 x 21 cm) and white
(13.8 x 9.5 cm) • Pattern 3 • 2 cm wide strips from
1 sheet of the red Iris folding paper set and from
2 purple and red envelopes • Silver holographic
paper • Diamond border ornament punch

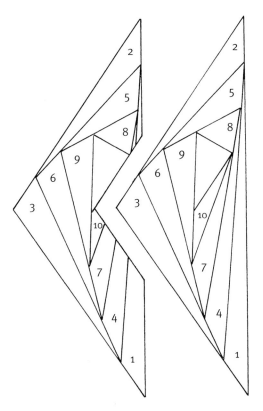

Pattern 3

Card 3

Card: pine green A339 (13 x 26 cm), dark blue A417 (12.3 x 12.3 cm) and white (10.8 x 10.8 cm) • Pattern 4 • 2 cm wide strips from 3 sheets of the blue and green Iris folding paper sets and from 2 blue envelopes • Silver deco tape • Flower mosaic punch

Card 4

Card: dark red (13 x 26 cm) and white (12 x 12 cm) • Piece of pink paper (12.4 x 12.4 cm) • Pattern 4 • 2 cm wide strips from 4 sheets of the blue, purple and red Iris folding paper sets • 1.6 cm wide strips from a red greetings sheet • Silver holographic paper • Heart border ornament punch

Card 5

Card: dark blue A417 (13 x 26 cm), billiard-table green (12.4 x 12.4 cm) and white (11.8 x 13 cm) • Pattern 4 • 2 cm wide strips from 5 sheets of the blue, green and petrol Iris folding paper sets • Silver holographic paper • Diamond border ornament punch
Cut the diamond out of the middle of the white card and decorate the edges using the border ornament punch.

Card 6

Card: white (14.8 x 21 cm and 11.5 x 9 cm) and royal blue A427 (12.8 x 9.4 cm) • Piece of blue Iris folding paper (13.6 x 9.7 cm) • Pattern 4 • 2 cm wide strips from 1 sheet of the blue Iris folding paper set, from 3 diferent blue envelopes and from 1 blue Iris folding greetings sheet • Silver holographic paper • Celestrial 3-in-1 corner punch

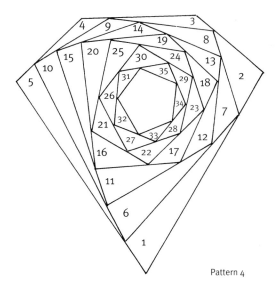

Pattern 4

1.

2.

3.

4.

5.

6.

7.

Baskets

A basket full of flowers, fruit or a good luck wish.

The basket is made according to the instructions given for card 1.

Card 1

Card: rust brown (14.8 x 21 cm) and white (13.8 x 9.5 cm) • Pattern 5 • 2 cm wide strips from 4 sheets of the orange Iris folding paper set • Gold holographic paper • Piece of bronze Iris folding paper (2 x 3 cm) from the yellow Iris folding paper set • Celestial 3-in-1 corner punch Cut the basket out of the white card and punch out the top corners. Fill the basket with the strips of paper. Cut the handle out of one of the strips of brown paper. Cut three pears out of bronze paper and stick everything in the basket.

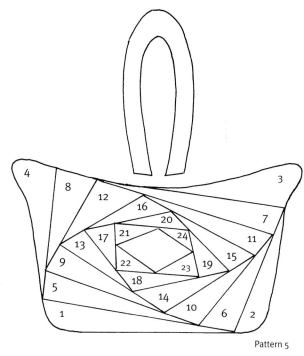

Pattern 5

Card 2

Card: Christmas green P18 (14.8 x 21 cm) and pearl grey C120 (14.3 x 9.8 cm) • Pattern 5 • 2 cm wide strips from 4 sheets of the green Iris folding paper set • Gold holographic paper • Flowers from the Flower 3-in-1 corner punch • Branch figure punch • Asian flower punch

Card 3

Card: green (14.8 x 21 cm), cream A241 (13.8 x 9.6 cm) and liver brown (13.5 x 9.4 cm) • Pattern 5 • 4 groups of 2 cm wide strips from 1 sheet of the green Iris folding paper set and from 2 green/brown envelopes • Gold holographic paper • Flower punch • Leaf mini distance punch • 3 glass jewels (Ornare MD)

Card 4

Card: green A309 (14.8 x 21 cm), cream A241 (14.1 x 10 cm) and honey yellow A243 (13.5 x 9.6 cm) • Pattern 5 • 2 cm wide strips from 1 sheet of the yellow Iris folding paper set and from 3 yellow/green envelopes • Gold holographic paper • Text sticker • Apples from the punch • Apple corner punch

Card 5

Card: nut brown P39 (14.8 x 21 cm) and cream Firenze (13.4 x 9.6 cm) • Pattern 5 • 4 groups of 2 cm wide strips from 3 sheets of the orange Iris folding paper set • Piece of bronze Iris folding paper (2 x 3 cm) for the pears • Gold holographic paper • Lily corner punch

Card 6

Card: rust brown (14.8 x 21 cm) and white (13.8 x 9.5 cm) • Pattern 5 • 2 cm wide strips from 2 sheets of the yellow Iris folding paper set and from 2 brown envelopes • Gold deco tape • Mushrooms from the hand punch • Leaves border ornament punch
Decorate the top corners of the white card with part of the border ornament punch and cut the basket out.

Card 7

Card: green (14.8 x 21 cm) and cream A241 (14.8 x 9.9 cm) • Pattern 5 • 2 cm wide strips from 2 sheets of the green Iris folding paper set and from 2 green envelopes • Green holographic paper • Text sticker • Leaves border ornament punch • Ivy punch

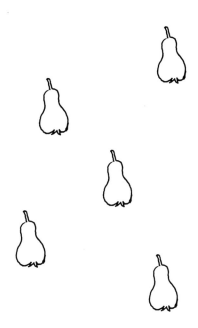

Cake

> *A party is not a party without a cake.*

All the cards are made according to the instructions given for card 1.

Card 1 (on the cover)

Card: crimson A549 (13 x 26 cm), yellow-pink C350 (12.2 x 12.2 cm) and lily white C110 (11.4 x 11.4 cm) • Pattern 6 • 2 cm wide strips from 2 sheets of the red and orange Iris folding paper sets • Orange holographic paper • Flower mosaic punch • Drop hand punch • Leaf distance punch

Cut both parts of the cake out of the small card and punch out the top corners. First fill the top half of the cake and then the bottom half with the *sponge fingers*. Use the light box to copy the dish onto orange paper. Cut it out and stick it under the cake. Stick the leaves on the front of the card on the strip between the two halves of the cake and on the 0.3 cm wide candles to make flames.

1.

3.

2.

4.

Card 2

Card: sienna yellow C374 (13 x 26 cm), metallic bronze P144 (12.2 x 12.2 cm) and white C335 (11.5 x 11.5 cm) • Pattern 6 • 2 cm wide strips from 2 sheets of the yellow and orange Iris folding paper sets • Gold holographic paper • Lace 3-in-1 corner punch

Card 3

Card: sunny yellow A247 (13 x 26 cm) and white (12 x 12 cm) • Pattern 6 • 2 cm wide strips from 4 different yellow and red envelopes • Gold deco tape • Drop hand punch • Hole punch • Leaves border ornament punch

Card 4

Card: iris blue P31 (13 x 26 cm) and white (11.7 x 11.7 cm) • Pattern 6 • 2 cm wide strips from 4 sheets of the purple Iris folding paper set • Piece of purple Iris folding paper (2.5 x 8 cm) for the bottom half of the cake • Silver deco tape • Stars from the punch • Victorian corner punch for the top of the cake • Flag from a blue greetings sheet • Celestial 3-in-1 corner punch
Punch out the top corners of the white card and fill the bottom half of the cake first.

Pattern 7a

Pattern 6

Rose

Roses and forget-me-nots are the best gifts.

The roses are filled in two different ways. Cards 2, 4 and 5 are made using pattern 7a and are filled in the usual way. Cards 1, 3 and 3 are made using pattern 7b and are filled by going round in a circle. Pay good attention to the numbering!

Card 1

Card: orange-brown (14.8 x 21 cm) and ivory (13.8 x 9.5 cm) • Pattern 7b • 2 cm wide strips from 7 different shades of orange origami paper • Piece of green paper (6 x 6 cm) for the stem and the leaf • Orange holographic paper • Text sticker • Celestial corner scissors

Cut the flower out of the white card and use the corner scissors to cut off the top corners. Take the darkest orange strips and use them to fill all the no. 1 sections. In other words, all the no. 1 sections are filled with the *same* colour. Use a lighter shade to fill the no. 2 sections. Use another shade to fill the no. 3 sections, etc. Cut the stem and the leaf out of green paper and stick them under the rose, together with the text sticker.

Card 2

Card: red (14.8 x 21 cm) and white (13.8 x 9.5 cm) • Pattern 7a • 2 cm wide strips from 5 sheets of the red Iris folding paper set • Piece of paper (6 x 6 cm) from the green Iris folding paper set for the stem and the leaf • Red holographic paper

Cut the flower out of the white card. Fill the pattern as described for the basic pattern.

Card 3

Card: red A517 (14.8 x 21 cm) and pale pink C103 (14.2 x 9.7 cm) • Pattern 7b • 7 groups of 2 cm wide strips from 2 sheets of the red Iris folding paper set and from 3 different red envelopes • Piece of green paper (6 x 6 cm) for the stem and the leaf • Red holographic paper • Corner and border embossing template

Cut the flower out of the pale pink card. Emboss the top and cut the small sections open.

Card 4

Card: white (14.8 x 21 cm and 13.8 x 9 cm) • Piece of green Iris folding paper (14.2 x 9.6 cm) • Pattern 7a • 2 cm wide strips from 5 sheets of the orange Iris folding paper set • Piece of paper (6 x 6 cm) from the green Iris folding paper set for the leaf and the stem • Gold deco tape • Multi-corner punch

Card 5

Card: purple P13 (14.8 x 21 cm) and cream C103
(13 x 9.1 cm) • Piece of pink paper (13.6 x 9.7 cm)
from the purple Iris folding paper set • Pattern 7a
• 2 cm wide strips from 5 sheets of the purple Iris
folding paper set • Piece of green paper (6 x 6 cm)
from the aqua Iris folding paper set for the stem
and the leaf • Lilac holographic paper • Text
sticker

Card 6

Card: white C335 (14.8 x 21 cm) and metallic P144
(14.8 x 10.3 cm) for a covering card • Pattern 7b •
7 groups of 2 cm wide strips from the yellow Iris
folding paper set and from different yellow
envelopes • Piece of petrol Iris folding paper
(6 x 6 cm) for the stem and the leaf • Gold deco
tape • Corner and border embossing template
(MD)
Cut the rose out of the front of the card. Embos
the border and cut out the triangles.

Pattern 7b

1.

2.

3.

4.

5.

6.

Spruces

Many variations using a single spruce.

Card 1

Card: Christmas green P18 (14.8 x 21 cm) and white (14 x 9.7 cm) • Pattern 8 • 1.5 cm wide strips from 3 sheets of the green Iris folding paper set • Gold holographic paper • Star, tree and Christmas embossing stencils • Green and gold aquarel pencil

Cut the spruce out of the back of the white card and emboss the stars, the spruces and the text. Fill the pattern with the strips of paper.

Card 2

Card: white (14.8 x 21 cm) and green (13.4 x 9.5 cm) • Pattern 8 • 1.5 cm wide strips from 3 different greyish white envelopes • Christmas vellum (10 x 6 cm) • 0.7 cm wide strips of green Iris folding greetings paper • Silver holographic paper

Cut the vellum paper diagonally through the middle and draw the diagonal lines on the green card. Cut the spruces out of the area between the two lines. Stick the vellum and the text strips on the card after completing the Iris folding.

Card 3

Card: Christmas green P18 (14.8 x 21 cm and 3 strips of 9.3 x 1 cm) and white (13.3 x 9.3 cm) •

Pattern 8 • 1.5 cm wide strips from 3 sheets of the petrol Iris folding paper set • Silver holographic paper • Spirelli card (ø 6.5 cm) with silver thread • Stars from the Star corner punch • Spruce photo corner figure punch

Card 4

Card: white (14.8 x 21 cm) and metallic green P143 (14.8 x 10.3 cm and 14.8 x 9 cm) • Pattern 8 • 1.5 cm wide strips from 3 sheets of the petrol Iris folding paper set • Gold deco tape • Holly template (Ornare MD)

Place the Ornare template against the inside of the white card and prick the holly. Fill the spruce with strips of paper. Stick the smallest green card behind the spruce and cut one side of the spruce out of the card. Prick the holly on the other green card and stick it on the right-hand half of the white card.

Card 5

Card: white (13 x 26 cm and 8.8 x 8.8 cm) and metallic green P143 (10.8 x 10.8 cm) • Pattern 8 • 1.5 cm wide strips from 3 sheets of the petrol Iris folding paper set • Gold holographic paper • Christmas stamp • Black ink-pad • Gold relief powder

Cut the spruce out of the smallest card and fill it with strips. Stamp around the spruce and sprinkle the powder on the wet ink. Shake the excess powder off. Warm the card, for example, over a toaster until the print becomes slightly raised and begins to sparkle.

Card 6

Card: white (13 x 26 cm and 6 x 4.2 cm) and Christmas green P18 (12.5 x 5 cm and 13 x 0.3 cm) • Pattern 8 • 1.5 cm wide strips from 3 sheets of the petrol Iris folding paper set • Silver holographic paper • Village embossing stencil • Spruce photo corner figure punch

Cut the spruce out of the small white card. Stick it on the green card after completing the Iris folding. Punch out the top and bottom right-hand corners of the double card. Stick the narrow strip on the left-hand side and the green card on the right-hand side and insert the corners into the photo corners.

Card 7

Card: white (13 x 26 cm and 12.5 x 12.5 cm) • Pattern 8 • 1.5 cm wide strips from 3 sheets of the green Iris folding paper set • Spruce embroidery pattern • Gold embroidery thread and 14 gold beads • Gold deco tape

Use a pencil to draw four squares (6 x 6 cm) with a 0.3 cm gap between each square on the left-hand side of the inside of the card. Cut the spruce out of the top left and bottom right-hand squares and fill them with strips. Copy the embroidery pattern in

the other squares. Embroider the spruce using a stem stich and sew the beads in place. Mark the edges of the squares with embroidery thread. Use the small card to decorate the card.

Card 8

Card: white (13 x 26 cm and a 9.5 x 9.5 x 13.4 cm triangle) and green P18 (11.2 x 12.3 cm) • Pattern 8 • 1.5 cm wide strips from 3 sheets of the petrol Iris folding paper set • Silver holographic paper • Spirelli card (ø 6 cm) with silver thread • Spruce photo corner figure punch

Cut the spruce in the white triangle and fill it with strips. Punch out the bottom right-hand corner of the green card. Stick the cards together. Stick the spruces on the Spirelli punch. Wind the thread around them and use glue to stick them in place. Punch out a separate photo corner from the top left-hand corner and decorate the corner with a spruce from the photo corner figure punch.

Pattern 8

Comets and Christmas decorations

You can make a wish when you see a

comet or a falling star.

The comet is made according to the description given for card 1 and the Christmas decoration is made according to the description given for card 4.

Card 1

Card: yellow R67 (14.8 x 21 cm) and iris blue P31 (14.3 x 9.7 cm) • Pattern 9 • 2 cm wide strips from gold paper of the red Iris folding paper set, from 2 different yellow envelopes and from blue Iris folding greetings paper • Gold holographic paper • Stars from the Celestial 3-in-1 corner punch • Star corner punch

Cut the star, except the tail, out of the blue card and punch out the corners. After completing the Iris folding, cut out two tails and stick them on the card together with some stars.

Card 2

Card: ice blue P42 (14.8 x 21 cm) and royal blue A427 (12.8 x 9.2 cm) • Pattern 9 • 2 cm wide strips from 4 sheets of the blue, aqua and purple Iris folding paper sets • Silver holographic paper • Celestial 3-in-1 corner punch

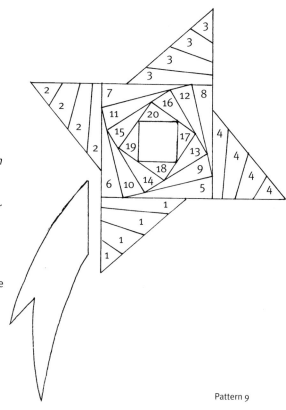

Pattern 9

Card 3

Card: violet P20 (14.8 x 21 cm) and dark blue A417 (13.8 x 9 cm) • Pattern 9 • 2 cm wide strips from the yellow Iris folding paper set, from 2 yellow and purple envelopes and from a sheet of blue Iris folding greetings paper • Silver holographic paper

Card 4

Card: iris blue P31 (13 x 26 cm) and white (12 x 12 cm) • Pattern 10 • 4 groups of 2 cm wide strips from 2 sheets of the purple Iris folding paper set • Piece of purple Iris folding paper (6 x 7 cm) for the top and bottom of the decoration • Silver holographic paper • Star border ornament punch
Cut 0.3 x 0.3 cm off the corners of the white card and punch out the stars. Cover the top and bottom of the Christmas decoration and then fill the middle section with strips. Cut out a hook and stick it on the card together with the stars.

Card 5

Card: white (13 x 26 cm) and purple P46 (10 x 10 cm) • Piece of de luxe silver Iris folding paper (11.2 x 11.2 cm) • Pattern 10 • 2 cm wide strips from 3 sheets of the purple Iris folding paper set and from 1 sheet of de luxe silver Iris folding paper • Piece of de luxe silver Iris folding paper

(6 x 7 cm) for the top and bottom of the Christmas decoration • Silver holographic paper

Card 6

Card: purple P13 (13 x 26 cm), purple P46 (12.5 x 12.5 cm) and white (11.5 x 11.5 cm) • Pattern 10 • 4 groups of 2 cm wide strips from 3 sheets of the purple Iris folding paper set • Piece of purple holographic paper (6 x 7 cm) for the top and bottom of the Christmas decoration • Silver holographic paper for the middle of the decoration and the hook • Star photo corner figure punch

Card 7

Card: white (14.8 x 21 cm and 13.8 x 9.4 cm) • Piece of paper (13.3 x 9.7 cm) from the purple Iris folding paper set • Pattern 10 • 2 cm wide strips from 4 sheets of the purple Iris folding paper set • Piece of paper (6 x 7 cm) from the purple Iris folding paper set for the top and bottom of the Christmas decoration • Silver holographic paper • Thread for the hook • Holly border ornament punch

Fold

¹/₂ of the hook

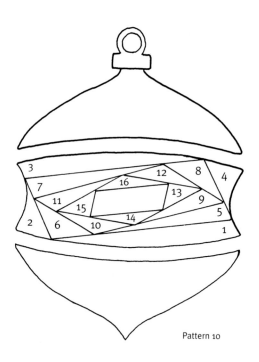

Pattern 10

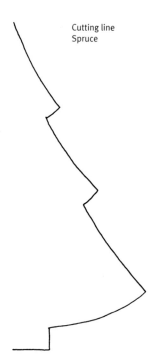

Cutting line
Spruce

Many thanks to:

Kars & Co B.V. in Ochten (the Netherlands) and Koninklijke Talens (card) in Apeldoorn (the Netherlands) for providing the materials.

The materials used can be ordered by shopkeepers from:
Kars & Co BV in Ochten, the Netherlands
Ecstasy Crafts, Shannonville, Canada
Search Press, Turnbridge Wells, United Kingdom